Who's Here?

Written by Linda Strachan

Illustrated by Wayne Ford

Who lives here?

2

Who lives here?

6

A spider lives in a web.

Spider

Web

Who lives here?

4

A bird lives in a nest.

Bird

Nest

nest   egg

3

Who lives here?

8

A snail lives in its shell.

7

Snail

snail   shell

Who lives here?

A squirrel lives in a drey.

Grey squirrel

Drey

13

Who lives here?

10

A rabbit lives in a burrow.

Rabbit

burrow   rabbit

9

Who lives here?

12

A fish lives in water.

Fish

Lake

water

11

15

Hedgehog

nest   hedgehog

Index

A hedgehog lives in a nest.